KB244187

Hidden Secrets of Famous Paintings

Happy House

About Wise & Wide

- A systematic 6-level English reading program based on Lexile® measures
- Diverse and interesting topics chosen from the elementary curriculums of Korea and English speaking western countries
- Well-written books in various forms including fiction stories, descriptive texts, and classics retold
- The informative but original fiction stories grab your interest, leading to the easy and clear understanding of the educational content.
- Improve thinking skills with solid after-reading activities at all levels of the series.

Wise & Wide is a 6-level English reading program that consists of 60 books and each level is systematically divided by Lexile® measures. The Lexile® Framework for Reading is the most popular reading measuring system in American formal education curriculums and many English programs. Over 20 out of 50 states in the U.S. mark Lexile® measures directly on students' final report cards and over 300 well-known publishers adopt and use Lexile® measures.

Experience many kinds of readings written by professional writers from the U.S. and England. They used interesting topics that were carefully chosen after analyzing elementary curriculums from around the world including Korea, the U.S., England, and Australia among many others. Comprehensive after-reading activities including graphic organizers, speaking tasks, and After-reading Tests are ready for you.

Levels in the series and their corresponding Lexile® measures

Level	Lexile® measures	U.S. Grade
Level 1	Below 200L	Pre K - K
Level 2	190L - 400L	Lower Grade 1
Level 3	350L - 530L	Upper Grade 1
Level 4	420L - 650L	Grade 2
Level 5	520L - 940L	Grade 3 - 4
Level 6	830L - 1070L	Grade 5 - 6

* Smart Readers: Wise & Wide level 1 is applicable to the preschool level in the U.S.
* The source of the relationship between Lexile® measures and U.S. school grades: CCSS(Common Core State Standards) FOR ENGLISH LANGUAGE ARTS, APPENDIX A (2012, which is used by 45 states in the U.S.)

Topic List

	Level 1	Level 2	Level 3	Level 4	Level 5	Level 6
Book 1	Science>Biology: The hibernation of animals Story	Science>Biology: Living and nonliving things Story	Science>Biology> Animals & the Environment: Sea otters Story	Environment> Living with nature: The diver & the persimmon tree Story	Science>Biology> Animal: Amazing animals of the Amazon Story	Science>Biology: Germs, transmitted diseases Story
Book 2	Literature> World classics: Aesop's fables Story	Literature> Traditional fairy tale: Old tales about stones Story	Social Studies> Economy: To run a business to make and save money Story	Science>Biology> Plants: Photosynthesis Story	Science>Earth science: Earth's layers, earthquakes, volcanoes, and earth's atmosphere Report	Mathematics> Sequence: The golden ratio & the Fibonacci sequence Story
Book 3	Science>Physics: How shadows are formed Story	Literature> World classics: Peter Pan Story	Science>Scientific technology: Nanobots Story	Literature>Myths: World's creation stories Story	Literature> Legend: The story of King Arthur Story	Literature>Myths: Constellation myths Story
Book 4	Literature> Traditional literature: The Talmud Story	Science>Biology> Animal: Polar bears Story	Science>Biology> Animal: Mountain gorillas Story	Social Studies> Cultural anthropology: Amazing ancient cultures of the world Story	Science> Earth science: Clouds and weather Story	Literature> Human & animals: The friendship between a girl and a horse Story
Book 5	Social Studies> Ethics: Rules in daily life Story	Science>Biology: The five senses Report	Social Studies> Cultural anthropology: Astonishing festivals Report	Art>Music: Stories from two operas Story	Social Studies> World culture & history: The Renaissance Story	Sports> Board sports: Surfing & snowboarding Story
Book 6	Social Studies> World geography & travel: Tourist attractions around the world Story	Science>Biology> Animal: Dinosaurs Story	Science> Astronomy: The solar system Story	Social Studies> People: Three great people who overcame hardships Story	Science>Scientific technology: The wonderful world of robots Report	Art>Music: Composers of the Romantic Era Report
Book 7	Science> Space science: The life of astronauts Report	Social Studies> Cultural anthropology: Mythological monsters from around the world Report	Mathematics> Elementary mathematics: Numbers, measurement, shapes and data Report	Science & Social Studies> Technology & culture: Inventions from around the world Report	Art>Works of art: Famous paintings Report	Social Studies> Human & animals: Animals in action for human Report
Book 8	Social Studies> Cultural anthropology: Various living cultures of the world Story	Art>Music: Instruments in the orchestra Story		Social Studies> History: The California Gold Rush Report	Social Studies & Science> Psychology: Psychology in everyday life Story	Literature> World classics: The Merchant of Venice Story
Book 9						
Book 10						

* 10 books in each level will be published.

How to Use This Book

• Before Reading

You can easily find the topic and what kind of story you are about to read.

• The text

All the stories were written by professional writers from the U.S. and England, so you will read authentic and appropriate English sentences and expressions in every book in the series.

• Pop Quiz

Check out right away if you understand what you have just read by solving a pop quiz that checks your comprehension.

• Key Words

The key words and expressions on each page are listed for you to easily study them.

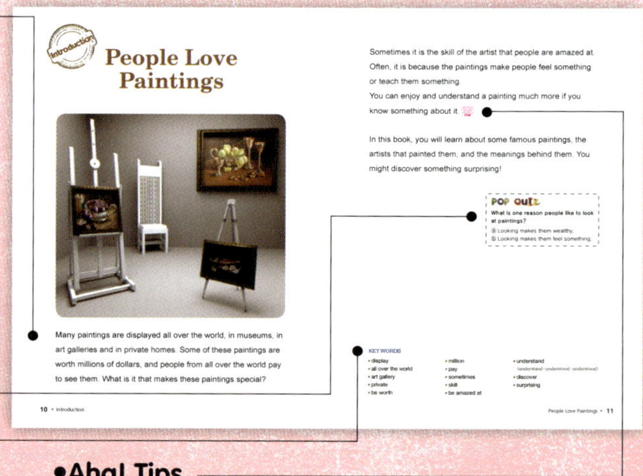

• Aha! Tips

Download free Korean explanations at *www.ihappyhouse.co.kr* for all of the sentences marked with "Aha!". These explain cultural, scientific, and economic knowledge or they deal with aspects of English such as grammatical structures or idiomatic expressions. There are lots of "Aha! Tips" to help you understand the text.

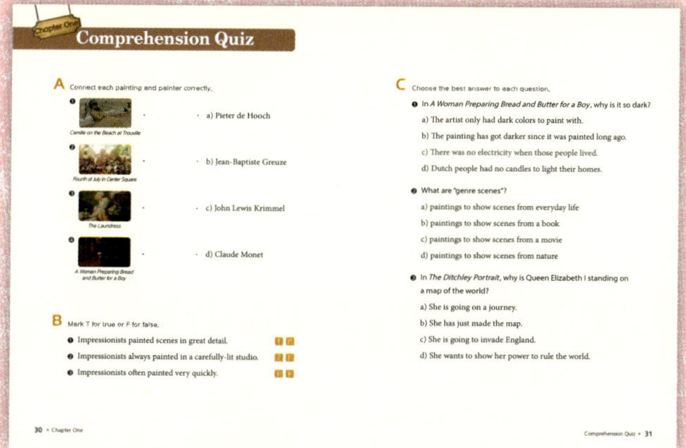

• Comprehension Quiz

After reading one chapter, solve various questions to find out if you fully understand the content.

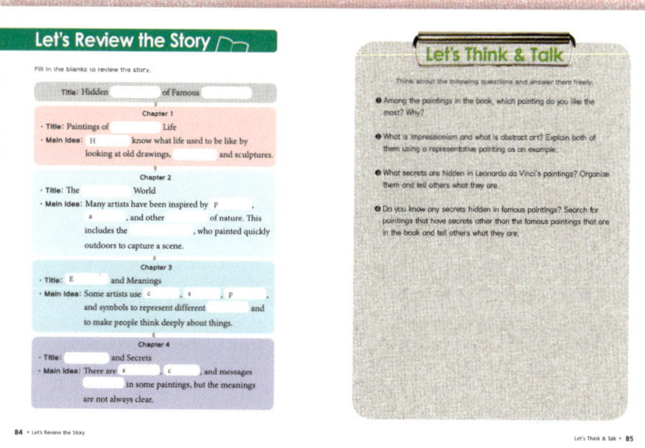

• Let's Review the Story /
• Let's Think & Talk

Fill in the blanks in the organizer to summarize the whole story. Express your own thinking and feelings about the story by answering the questions. You can build up logic and reasoning skills for your essay examinations in the future.

Appendix

Audio CD

In the CD audio book form, the texts are read vividly by American professional voice actors.
(MP3 files downloaded for free)

After-reading Test

Solve an additionally provided After-reading Test for each book.

The Korean translation, Answer Keys, a Word Quiz, a Word List, and Aha! Tips for each book

You can download them for free at *www.ihappyhouse.co.kr* or *www.darakwon.co.kr*

Before Reading

Hidden Secrets of Famous Paintings

Level 5–7,
Lexile®850L

•Art>Works of art
•Report

Peeking into the secrets hidden in famous paintings!

There is a movie called *The Da Vinci Code*. It is a movie that described the process of decoding secret codes hidden in Leonardo da Vinci's paintings in order to solve a murder case that took place in the Louvre Museum in Paris, France. You might find new and interesting facts unexpectedly while appreciating a painting if you don't just look at the painter's painting style (the way the painter painted) or painting materials but also search for the painter's thoughts and secrets hidden inside.

In the book, we will take a close look at the things hidden in various famous paintings. Each painting reflects a specific painting style at that time it was painted. Looking for hidden secrets is a good way to make famous paintings more interesting.

Summary

There are paintings that realistically show how people lived at the time they were painted. These paintings are called "genre scenes." On the other hand, there are famous painters that used a painting style called "Impressionism" in which they painted their overall impression and fleeting feelings.

Then there are painters who captured the various faces of nature such as animals, plants, mountains, etc. They portrayed the beauty of nature delicately. In contrast, there are paintings that show human emotions symbolically using lines, colors, etc. This style is called "abstract art."

Finally, there are famous paintings that contain profound secrets. *Mona Lisa* and *The Last Supper* by Leonardo da Vinci are two of the most typical examples.

Contents

Hidden Secrets of Famous Paintings

2 About Wise & Wide
4 How to Use This Book
6 Before Reading

Introduction / Chapter One
10 People Love Paintings
12 Paintings of Everyday Life
30 Comprehension Quiz

Chapter Two
32 The Natural World
46 Comprehension Quiz

Chapter Three
48 Emotions and Meanings
68 Comprehension Quiz

Chapter Four
70 Codes and Secrets
82 Comprehension Quiz

84 Let's Review the Story
85 Let's Think & Talk
86 Let's Review the Story (Answers)
87 After-reading Test

Hidden Secrets of
Famous Paintings

Introduction

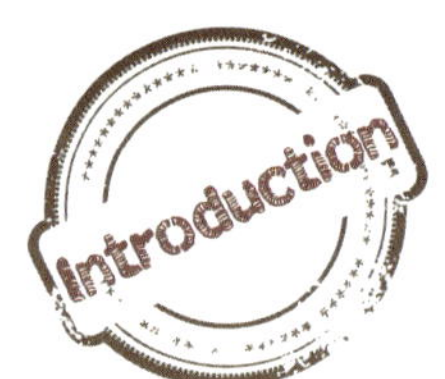

People Love Paintings

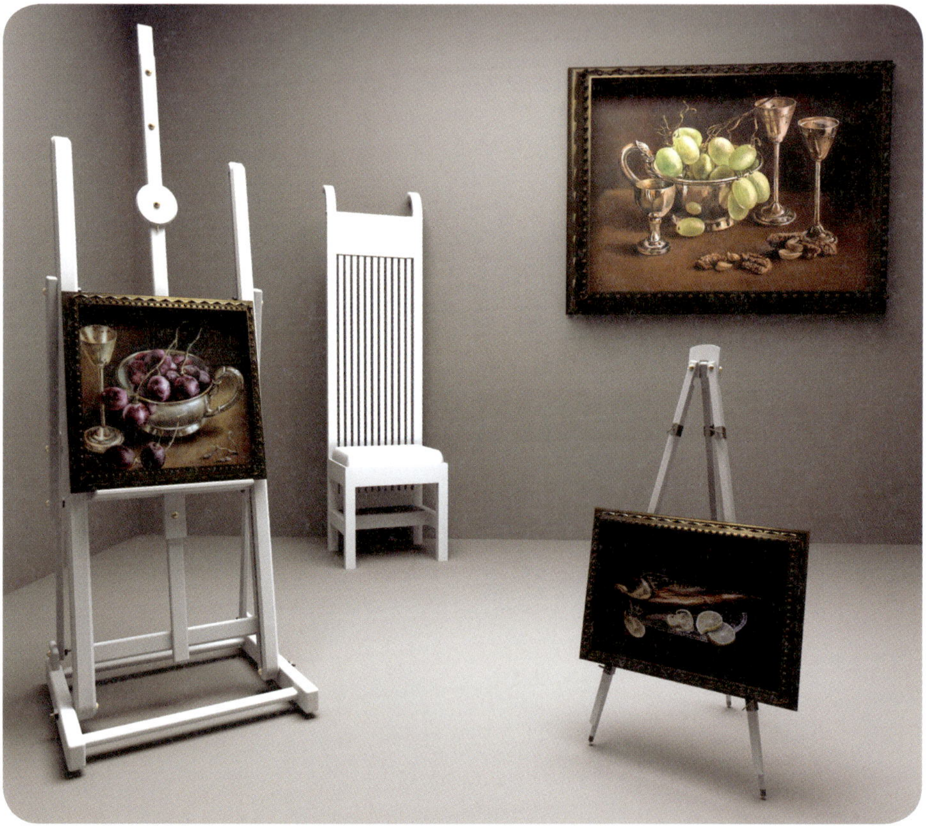

Many paintings are displayed all over the world, in museums, in art galleries and in private homes. Some of these paintings are worth millions of dollars, and people from all over the world pay to see them. What is it that makes these paintings special?

Sometimes it is the skill of the artist that people are amazed at.

Often, it is because the paintings make people feel something

or teach them something.

You can enjoy and understand a painting much more if you

know something about it. 

In this book, you will learn about some famous paintings, the

artists that painted them, and the meanings behind them. You

might discover something surprising!

KEY WORDS

- display
- all over the world
- art gallery
- private
- be worth
- million
- pay
- sometimes
- skill
- be amazed at
- understand
  (understand-understood-understood)
- discover
- surprising

Paintings of Everyday Life

How do historians know what people wore in past times? How
do they know how people dressed their hair?

There were no photographs taken until the nineteenth century.

In fact, the first photograph to include humans was taken in

Paris, in 1838.

This means that all the information about how people looked

before this time has been gained by looking at drawings,

paintings and sculptures.

KEY WORDS

- historian
- **wear** (wear-wore-worn)
- in past times
- dress one's hair
- **photograph** (*cf.* photographer)
- **take** (take-took-taken)
- century

- in fact
- include
- **mean** (mean-meant-meant)
- information
- gain
- drawing
- sculpture

▲ the first photograph to include humans

This painting is called *A Woman Preparing Bread and Butter for a Boy*. It was painted around 1660 by a Dutch artist called Pieter de Hooch. The original painting can be seen in the J. Paul Getty Museum in Los Angeles, U.S.A.

You might be surprised to learn that the younger figure in the picture is a boy! He is wearing an outfit that looks like a dress, and his hair is long and girlish. He is holding a wide-brimmed hat. But this shows us what Dutch boys wore in those days.

The picture is very dark, which reminds us that there was no electricity then. The only light was candlelight, and candles were saved for use when it was really dark.

This scene takes place when there is daylight, so the door is open to let the light in.

KEY WORDS

- prepare
- bread and butter
- around
- Dutch
- original
- surprised
- figure
- outfit
- girlish
- **hold** (hold-held-held)

- wide-brimmed
- in those days
- remind
- electricity
- candlelight (*cf.* candle)
- save
- scene
- take place
- daylight
- let in

There is a clue in the painting that tells us why the woman is preparing bread and butter for the boy.

There is a building just across the street, beyond the open door. There is a sign on that building which says *schole*. This means "school."

So the boy is getting ready to go to school, and the woman is preparing some food for him to take.

There is no fancy lunchbox, no meat or fruit and certainly no junk food such as chips or cookies! His food is very plain.

KEY WORDS

- clue
- across
- beyond
- sign
- get ready to + *Verb* (get-got-gotten/got)
- fancy
- lunchbox
- certainly
- junk food
- such as
- chip
- plain
- daily
- laundress

Another picture that shows the daily life
of working people is The Laundress.

▲ Jean-Baptiste Greuze's self-portrait

It was painted by French artist Jean-Baptiste Greuze in 1761.

At this time, people did not do their own washing, but sent it to a laundress. She did not have a modern washing machine and everything had to be done by hand. You can see from this painting that she had a bowl of water. It contained a type of detergent to clean the clothes.

She had to make the detergent herself. It was not as good as modern detergents, so the laundress had to work hard to get the dirt out of clothes and bedding.

KEY WORDS

- French
- do the washing (do-did-done)
- modern
- washing machine
- contain
- a type of
- detergent
- get ... out of ~
- dirt (cf. dirty)
- bedding

There is a jug next to her. This probably contained clean, hot water to soak the clothes for several hours.

There was no way to dry the clothes except by squeezing out the water by hand and then hanging them up. You can see the laundry hanging behind the laundress. There is also a copper pot in which she made the detergent.

You can also see the style of clothing that working women wore in those days. She wears a cap to keep her hair out of the way, and long skirts with high heels. This type of clothing was not very practical for doing difficult, dirty work like this!

KEY WORDS

- jug
- next to
- probably
- soak
- several
- except
- squeeze out
- **hang up** (hang-hung-hung)

- laundry
- copper
- pot
- cap
- **keep ~ out of the way** (keep-kept-kept)
- high heel
- practical

Paintings that show scenes of everyday life are sometimes known as "genre scenes."

One of America's first painters of genre scenes was John Lewis Krimmel. He was born in Germany in 1786, but moved to the U.S.A. in 1809.

At this time, many black people in the U.S.A. were slaves. But there were also black people who were free members of society. Krimmel was one of the first artists to paint free black people. This painting, called *Fourth of July in Center Square*, was painted in 1819. It shows people celebrating in the city of Philadelphia.

The Fourth of July is still an important celebration in the U.S.A. It reminds people of the time when the U.S.A. became an independent nation. In modern times, there are parties and fireworks.

In this picture, you can see that the people are celebrating with music and dancing, food and drink, just as they do today!

The two men in the center of the picture are soldiers. They are celebrating with merchants who sell things and ordinary people who are just enjoying the celebration.

Most of the people in the painting are white. This tells us that black people were not always included in public life.

▲ the United States Declaration of Independence

KEY WORDS

- be known as
  (know-knew-known)
- genre scenes
- be born
- Germany
- move to

- slave
- society
- celebrate (*cf.* celebration)
- independent
- nation
- fireworks

- just as
- merchant
- ordinary
- public

Many wealthy people paid artists to paint their portraits, in the same way that modern celebrities might ask photographers to take their pictures. This was their way of showing how wealthy they were, so they made sure to wear their best clothes.

This famous portrait is known as *The Ditchley Portrait*. It shows English queen Elizabeth I. It was painted by Marcus Gheeraerts the Younger in 1592.

In it, the queen is standing on a map of the world, with her feet on England. This was done to show that she had power to rule the world from her kingdom.

You can see that her clothing is very grand. She wears a wide skirt and puffed sleeves, with a stiff lace ruff at her neck.

All these things make her appear to be bigger and more powerful than she would naturally be. The dress is richly patterned and her hair appears to be full of jewels.

KEY WORDS

- wealthy
- portrait
- in the same way
- celebrity
- make sure
- the Younger
- rule
- kingdom
- grand
- puffed sleeve
- stiff
- lace
- ruff
- appear
- naturally
- richly
- patterned
- be full of
- jewel

All of these paintings, and many others like them, show people and places painted in great detail.

However, there is a famous style of art called *Impressionism*, which shows scenes from real life in a different way. 🌐

Artists who painted in this way knew that when people see a new scene, they don't focus on one particular face or detail. Instead, they take in the whole scene. They look at the light, the colors, the movement, and the general activity that is going on. They get an *impression* of that moment.

This is what the artists tried to show in their paintings.

KEY WORDS

- **in detail** (*cf.* detail)
- **Impressionism** (*cf.* Impressionist)
- **focus on**
- **particular**
- **instead** (*cf.* instead of)
- **take in**
- **general** (*cf.* generally)
- **go on** (go-went-gone)
- **get an impression** (*cf.* impression)
- **carefully-lit**
- **studio**
- **more like**
- **snapshot**
- **capture**

There are several famous artists who were known as *Impressionists*. They include Monet, van Gogh, Renoir, Manet and Degas.

They often painted quickly outside instead of taking several days or weeks to paint in a carefully-lit studio. This means that their paintings were more like modern "snapshots" of everyday life. They captured a single moment.

▲ *Haystacks* by Claude Monet

▲ *Dance at Le Moulin de la Galette* by Pierre-Auguste Renoir

▲ *The Luncheon on the Grass* by Edouard Manet

▲ *Dancer with a Bouquet of Flowers* by Edgar Degas

This painting is called *Camille on the Beach at Trouville*. It was painted by Claude Monet in 1870.

Monet painted it while he was with his wife, Camille. They went on a vacation to the coast shortly after their marriage.

Camille is the woman in the pale dress, holding a sunshade. Experts who have studied this painting and others painted at the same time know that some of it was painted on the beach. There are grains of sand caught in the paint!

The painting gives us the impression that it is quite windy on the beach. The sea is not calm, but quite rough.

▲ a picture of Claude Monet

KEY WORDS

- while
- go on a vacation
- coast
- shortly after
- marriage
- pale
- sunshade

- expert
- at the same time
- grain
- quite
- windy
- calm
- rough

Camille has a scarf over her nose and mouth, which may be to keep the sand out. 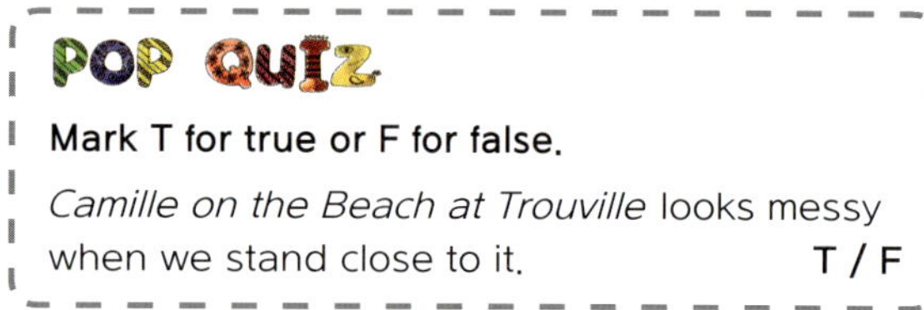

Camille's dress is almost the same color as the sand, so Monet has used thick strokes of white paint to show its lighter color. Many artists smooth these strokes together, but the Impressionists did not.

The painting may look quite messy if you stand close to it. But from a distance, the colors all smooth together. You can see this effect more clearly if you look at the boy in the background. Close up, the painting is made up of rough strokes. But from a distance, all the colors smooth together.

> ## POP QUIZ
> **Mark T for true or F for false.**
> *Camille on the Beach at Trouville* looks messy when we stand close to it.   T / F

KEY WORDS

- keep ~ out
- stroke
- lighter
- smooth

- messy
- from a distance (*cf.* distance)
- effect
- clearly

- background
- close up
- be made up of

Chapter One

Comprehension Quiz

A Connect each painting and painter correctly.

Camille on the Beach at Trouville

Fourth of July in Center Square

The Laundress

A Woman Preparing Bread
and Butter for a Boy

a) Pieter de Hooch

b) Jean-Baptiste Greuze

c) John Lewis Krimmel

d) Claude Monet

B Mark T for true or F for false.

❶ Impressionists painted scenes in great detail. T F

❷ Impressionists always painted in a carefully-lit studio. T F

❸ Impressionists often painted very quickly. T F

C Choose the best answer to each question.

❶ In *A Woman Preparing Bread and Butter for a Boy*, why is it so dark?

a) The artist only had dark colors to paint with.

b) The painting has got darker since it was painted long ago.

c) There was no electricity when those people lived.

d) Dutch people had no candles to light their homes.

❷ What are "genre scenes"?

a) paintings to show scenes from everyday life

b) paintings to show scenes from a book

c) paintings to show scenes from a movie

d) paintings to show scenes from nature

❸ In *The Ditchley Portrait*, why is Queen Elizabeth I standing on a map of the world?

a) She is going on a journey.

b) She has just made the map.

c) She is going to invade England.

d) She wants to show her power to rule the world.

The Natural World

Many painters choose the natural world as their subject. This is particularly common in Japanese art.

There are many beautiful paintings featuring birds, plants and mountains. Mount Fuji, a sacred mountain in Japan, is often included.

One of the best known Japanese paintings features something that is difficult to capture in paint — a moving wave!

The Great Wave off Kanagawa was painted by Katsushika Hokusai around 1830.

KEY WORDS

- natural world
- subject
- particularly
- common
- Japanese
- feature
- Mount Fuji
- sacred
- snow-capped
- open sea
- at first glance
- career
- sketch
- at the age of
- much good
- lifetime
- practice

The snow-capped mountain in the background is Mount Fuji.

The wave is out in the open sea off Japan.

At first glance, the mountain looks like part of the ocean, or the wave looks like a mountain with snow on it. But when you look more closely, you will see that there are also three boats in the picture.

It is said that Hokusai began his artistic career by sketching things at the age of five. But he didn't think that his pictures were much good until he reached the age of seventy, after a lifetime of practice!

Many Chinese paintings also include scenes from nature.

A Thousand Li of Rivers and Mountains was painted over a thousand years ago by a Chinese artist named Wang Ximeng. A "li" is a traditional Chinese unit of measurement. One li is the same as 500 meters, so a thousand li would be a distance of 500 km.

This painting shows everything you might have seen across 500 km of ancient China. The first things you notice are the mountain peaks and the lower green fields. Then there are lakes, bridges, ships, villages and people.

KEY WORDS

- Chinese
- traditional
- unit
- measurement
- ancient
- notice
- peak
- lower
- village

There is so much to look at in this painting, and since the real thing is 12 m long, it would take a long time to find all the details!

It is part of the art collection in the Palace Museum of Beijing. Wang Ximeng finished this amazing painting when he was only eighteen years old. He was a student of the Imperial Painting Academy and was taught by the Emperor himself. Unfortunately, he died in his early twenties.

KEY WORDS

- since
- collection
- palace
- finish

- imperial
- academy
- teach (teach-taught-taught)
- emperor

- unfortunately
  (↔ fortunately)
- early

Animals are a popular subject for painters. *Tiger in a Tropical Storm (Surprised)* by Henri Rousseau is especially well known.

KEY WORDS

- popular
- tropical
- especially
- well known (*cf.* well-known)

Why do you think the alternate title is "Surprised"? Is it the tiger that is surprised by the sudden flash of lightning? Or is there something hidden in the long grass that is surprised by the tiger pouncing on it?

The tiger appears to be looking off to the right of the picture. Its prey must be there.

You might think that the painter spent a lot of time in the jungle, studying tropical plants and experiencing wild storms. In fact, it is believed that Henri Rousseau never left his home country of France!

Many of the plants in the picture were probably seen in the Botanical Gardens of Paris. There were also examples of stuffed tigers for him to look at.

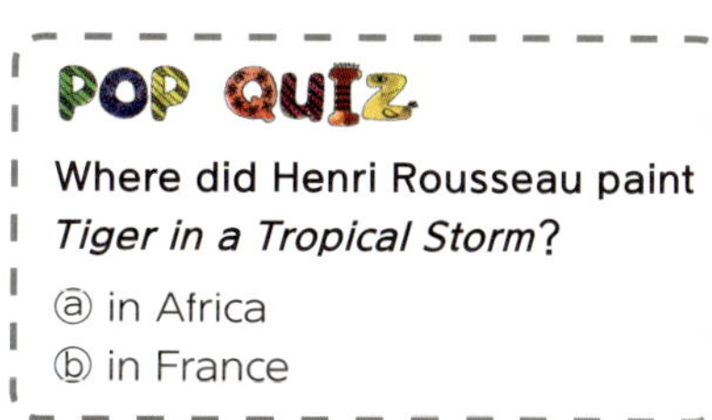

KEY WORDS

- alternate
- sudden
- flash
- lightning
- hidden (*cf.* hide (hide-hid-hidden))
- pounce on
- look off to
- prey

- must
- spend (spend-spent-spent)
- experience
- leave (leave-left-left)
- one's home country
- botanical garden
- stuffed

Of course, it is difficult to show the wildness of a storm in a non-moving picture. But Rousseau trailed silver paint diagonally across the picture. This gives the impression of rain.

Looking at this picture, it is easy to imagine the trees waving around in the wind, and the thunder booming in the darkened sky.  Aha!

How did Rousseau show rain in his painting?
ⓐ He put water on the picture.
ⓑ He put silver paint on the picture.

KEY WORDS

- wildness
- non-moving
- trail
- diagonally

- wave around
- thunder
- boom
- darkened

Another artist who put together small details to make one big picture is Hans Hoffmann of Germany. He painted *A Hare in the Forest* around 1585.

KEY WORDS

▪ put together   ▪ **hare** (*cf.* hare/hares)   ▪ forest

There are lots of clues that tell us this is not a real scene.

Hare are rarely seen sitting still like this — certainly not long enough for an artist to paint a picture!

Also, there are many other creatures pictured here that would not all gather in one place at the same time. There is a butterfly, a snail, and a lizard well camouflaged against the ground. You might have to look closely to find them all!

It seems likely that Hoffmann made lots of sketches of different plants and animals in the countryside near his home. Then, he took all these smaller drawings and put them together to make a complete painting. In this way, he was able to choose exactly what to put in the picture and where to put it so that it would be pleasing to look at.

KEY WORDS

- rarely
- still
- creature
- gather
- snail
- lizard

- camouflage
- likely
- countryside
- complete
- be able to + *Verb*
- pleasing

There is a whole area of art that is dedicated to painting plants. This is called *botanical art*, since botany is a study of plants.

Botanical artists paint a flower or plant exactly as it is. Their early works were often made into books so that other people could identify different types of plants. There were two Austrian men who are regarded by experts as the best botanical artists that ever lived. They lived around two hundred years ago, and their names were Franz and Ferdinand Bauer.

▲ an example of botanical art

- be dedicated to
- botanical art
- botany
- as it is

- identify
- Austrian
- regard A as B
- that ever lived

Franz Bauer was English king George III's botanical painter. He was invited to draw all the new flowering plants in the world-famous Kew Gardens in London, England. He looked at the plants so closely that people could see the different stages of their life cycles for the first time, without using a microscope. His brother, Ferdinand, was the botanical artist on a very famous voyage. The ship was called HMS Investigator, and the captain was Matthew Flinders.

You might think that there are not many plants to draw on board a sailing ship, but this ship went to Australia. It was a country that was full of new and astonishing things to discover! This was the first time that anyone had sailed all the way around Australia.

KEY WORDS

- invite
- stage
- life cycle
- for the first time
- without
- microscope
- voyage

- investigator
- captain
- on board a ship
- sailing ship
- astonishing
- sail
- all the way

- detailed
- including
- Banksia
- scarlet
- scientific

Ferdinand Bauer painted very detailed pictures of over a thousand plants, including Australia's well-known *Banksia*. This picture is called *Banksia coccinea*, which means "scarlet Banksia."

The *Banksia coccinea* painting is very scientific. It helps people to see exactly what the different parts of the plant look like.

Edouard Manet was a French painter who was suffering from a long illness in 1882. During that year, he painted this picture of a vase of flowers from a lilac tree. It is called *Lilac in a Glass*.

KEY WORDS

- suffer from
- illness
- during
- vase
- lilac

One of Manet's friends brought these flowers to his home as he lay ill in bed.

He was interested in the way the light traveled through the water and the glass. It made the lilac stems look as though they were bent. He carefully painted the stems in the water, and used different colors to show the light.

The very dark background behind the white and green stems was probably not real. Manet painted it on purpose, to show the difference between darkness and light. Perhaps because he thought that he was going to die.

Not long after this painting was finished, his left leg had to be removed and he died a year later.

POP QUIZ

How did the lilac stems look in the water?

ⓐ They looked as if they were bent.
ⓑ They looked longer than usual.

KEY WORDS

- **bring** (bring-brought-brought)
- **lie ill in bed** (lie-lay-lain)
- **be interested in** (*cf.* interest)
- **stem**
- **as though**
- **bend** (bend-bent-bent)
- **carefully**

- **on purpose**
- **difference**
- **between A and B**
- **darkness**
- **perhaps**
- **remove**

Comprehension Quiz

A The following sentences are about *Tiger in a Tropical Storm*. Fill in each blank with the right word below.

thunder	jungle	storm	tiger

❶ The ___________ appears to be looking off to the right of the picture.

❷ It is easy to imagine the trees waving around in the wind and the ___________ booming in the sky.

❸ You might think that the painter spent a lot of time in the ___________.

❹ It is difficult to show the wildness of a ___________ in a non-moving picture.

B These are explanations of Edouard Manet. Circle the right word for each underlined part.

❶ Edouard Manet was a (German / French / English) Impressionist painter.

❷ Manet painted a picture of a (bowl / cup / vase) of lilac flowers.

❸ Not long after the painting was finished, Manet's (bed / leg / hand) was removed.

C Choose the best answer to each question.

❶ How did Hokusai begin his artistic career?

a) by taking photographs of things

b) by making statues of things

c) by painting pictures of things

d) by sketching things

❷ How do we know that *A Hare in the Forest* is not a real scene? Choose two answers.

a) A hare would not live near a forest.

b) All the different creatures would not be close together at the same time.

c) A hare would not sit still and let itself be painted.

d) Butterflies and snails would not live in the same place.

❸ Why did Franz Bauer paint plants so carefully?

a) So that scientists could study them using a microscope.

b) So that people could understand the different stages of a plant's life cycle.

c) So that the king could hang the pictures in his palace.

d) So that he could take the pictures to show people in Australia.

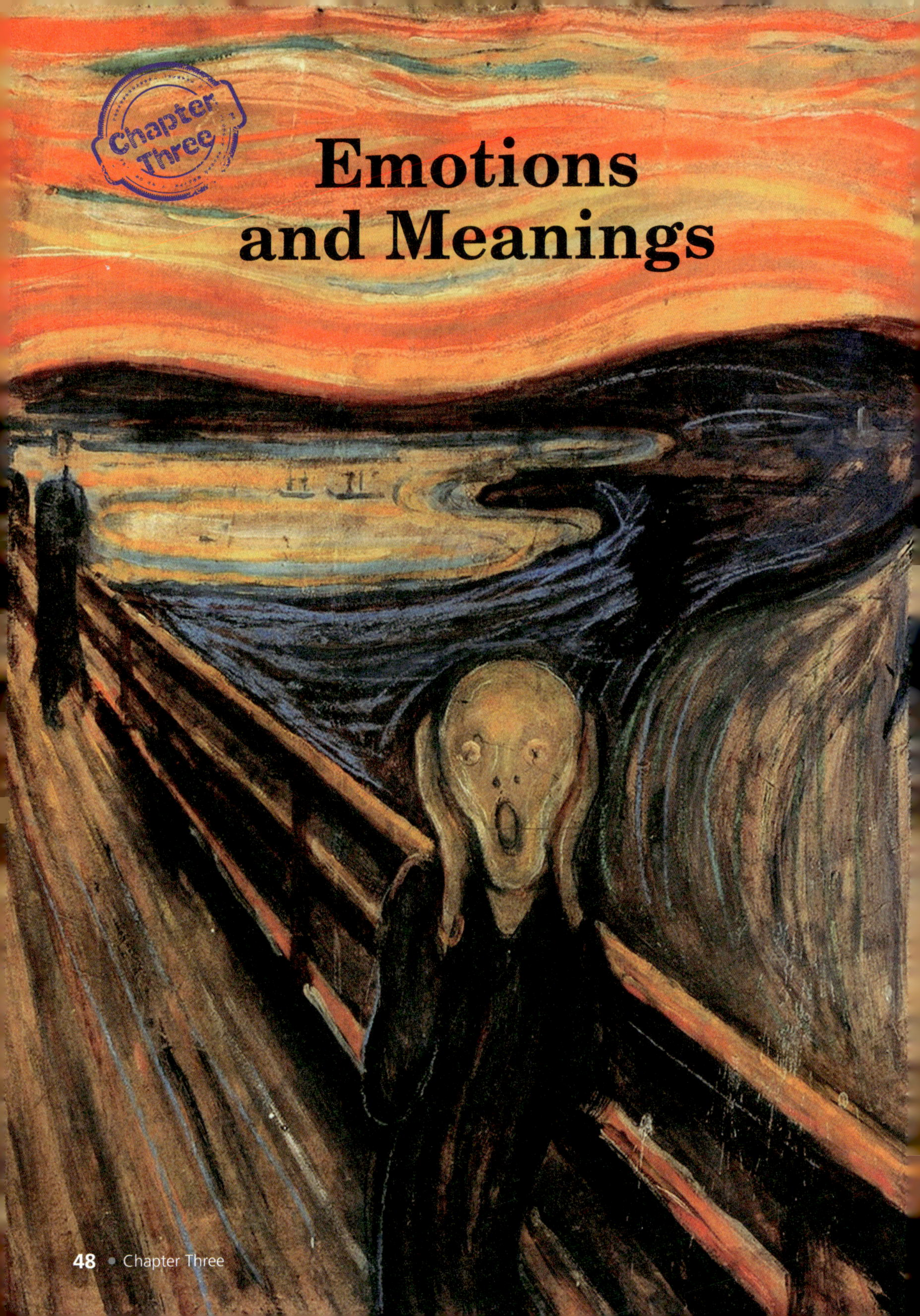

Emotions and Meanings

Sometimes a painting is simply a picture of something in real life. It is pleasant to look at, and the skill of the artist is displayed for everyone to see.

However, many paintings have a much deeper meaning. They represent different emotions, or they want to give a message to the people who view them.

A very famous painting about emotions is *The Scream*, by Norwegian artist Edvard Munch.

Painted in between 1893 and 1910, *The Scream* is actually a collection of four similar paintings. One of these was sold at a U.S. auction in 2012 for the incredible sum of $120 million!

KEY WORDS

- emotion
- simply
- pleasant
- deeper
- represent
- view
- scream
- Norwegian
- actually
- similar
- sell (sell-sold-sold)
- auction
- incredible
- sum

▲ four versions of *The Scream*

So what is this picture about? Who is the person at the front of the painting? Why is he holding his head in such a way? What has upset him so much?

He seems to be walking across a bridge or some kind of boardwalk. There is water swirling beneath, with a red sky above.

Munch's original title for the collection of paintings was *The Scream of Nature*, and perhaps this gives us a clue.

Fortunately for us, Munch kept a diary, in which he wrote about his inspiration for these paintings. He later turned this into a poem, which he painted onto the frame of one of the four paintings:

"I was walking along the road with two friends. The sun was setting. Suddenly the sky turned blood red. I paused, feeling exhausted, and leaned on the fence. There was blood and tongues of fire above the blue-black fjord and the city. My friends walked on, and I stood there trembling with anxiety, and I sensed an infinite scream passing through nature."

So we can see that this picture represents how anxious and tired the artist was feeling. He was overwhelmed by what he saw in nature.

KEY WORDS

- **upset** (upset-upset-upset)
- **boardwalk**
- **swirling**
- **beneath**
- **above**
- **keep a diary**
- **inspiration**
- **turn A into B**
- **poem**

- **frame**
- **along**
- **set** (set-set-set)
- **suddenly**
- **blood red** (*cf.* blood)
- **pause**
- **exhausted**
- **lean**
- **tongues of fire**

- **blue-black**
- **fjord**
- **tremble**
- **with anxiety**
- **sense**
- **infinite**
- **anxious**
- **overwhelm**

An equally famous — but more cheerful — painting is
Sunflowers by Vincent van Gogh. 🌐 He was one of the
Impressionist painters.

This Dutch artist must have liked sunflowers, because he painted seven different versions of this picture.

For van Gogh, yellow represented happiness.

The sunflower was also a symbol of devotion and loyalty. It represented the human soul, and some experts think that the flowers in his painting show the different stages of life and death. Some of the sunflowers still have lots of petals, but others have lost most of them and are drooping.

▲ Vincent van Gogh's self-portrait

KEY WORDS

▪ equally	▪ happiness	▪ petal
▪ cheerful	▪ devotion	▪ lose (lose-lost-lost)
▪ sunflower	▪ loyalty (*cf.* loyal)	▪ droop
▪ version	▪ soul	

This painting is called *Woman Reading a Letter*. It was completed around 1665 by another Dutch artist called Gabriel Metsu. It has many hidden meanings in it.

If you look closely at the woman's forehead, you will see that the hair has been plucked away. This was the fashion at that time. But there is a single curl left. This means that she is engaged to be married.

There is also a thimble on the floor at the front of the picture. This suggests that the woman was sewing when she received the letter. She has been distracted from her task by the importance of the letter. From this, we may guess that she has received a letter from her sweetheart.

The dog is a symbol of faithfulness, showing that she is loyal to her lover. But its excitement tells us that although the woman doesn't show it, she is excited too.

KEY WORDS

- forehead
- pluck away
- fashion
- curl
- be engaged to be married
- thimble
- suggest
- **sew** (*cf.* sewing)
- receive

- distract
- task
- importance
- guess
- sweetheart
- faithfulness
- lover
- excitement
- although

The mirror behind the woman's head reflects the window. It is in a simple wooden frame instead of a fancy silver one. This reminds us that we should not be too concerned with our looks.

The servant, who is holding another letter ready to post, has uncovered a painting of a ship on a stormy sea. This represents the difficulties of being in love when the two people are apart. There are other symbols here, too.

There is an abandoned shoe on the floor, and some laundry or sewing spilling out of a basket. What do you think the artist meant to say when he included these in the picture? Perhaps it means that although the woman looks calm on the outside, she is disturbed on the inside.

KEY WORDS

- reflect
- be concerned with
- looks
- servant
- post
- uncover
- difficulty
- be in love (with)

- apart
- abandoned
- spill
- mean to + *Verb*
- on the outside (↔ on the inside)
- disturbed (*cf.* disturbance)
- accompany

Metsu painted a second picture, *Man Writing a Letter*, to accompany this one. It shows the other half of the story.

▲ globe

The silver inkstand tells us that this man is wealthy. The globe in the corner suggests that he has traveled to different places.

The rug on the table is an expensive Turkish one, and it is wrinkled. This suggests that the man's mind is not calm. He is excited or disturbed by the writing of the letter.

As in the first painting, there is a picture within this picture. This time, it is a picture of a tree, which suggests something long lasting and secure.

In *Man Writing a Letter*, what is in the painting on the wall?
ⓐ a picture of a ship
ⓑ a picture of a tree

KEY WORDS

- inkstand
- globe
- in the corner
- rug
- expensive
- Turkish
- wrinkled
- lasting
- secure

Another painting with symbols that have a deep meaning is *The Ambassadors*. It was painted by Hans Holbein in 1533.

An ambassador is someone who represents his or her country and its people when they are in a foreign land.

On the left is the man who was the French ambassador to England in 1533. The man on the right is his friend, another ambassador and a bishop.

Now that you know more about the symbols in paintings, you might be able to guess what some of them mean.

There are two globes, one showing the earth and another that is related to the stars. This shows that they were interested in exploring. They liked to make new discoveries about science and the world around them.

There are some musical instruments, including a stringed instrument called a lute. There is also an open hymn book, suggesting an interest in religion.

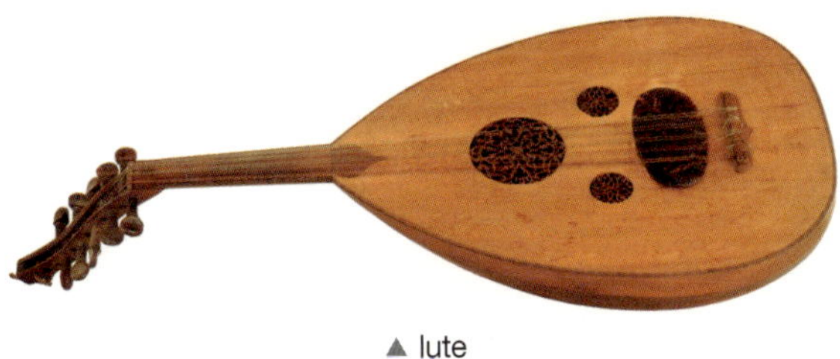

▲ lute

But what is the strange object in the lower part of the picture? It looks as though the artist has spilled paint on the canvas. This is a puzzle that can only be solved if you walk up to the canvas and view it from one side. Then, the strange object looks like this:

Artists often painted skulls or other symbols of death into their pictures, to remind people that they would not live forever.

Most of the paintings we have looked at are easy to understand if we look closely. They show people, places, animals, objects, or scenes of nature. But there are some types of art where the meaning is more difficult to understand.

Abstract art does not show a person, a place or an object that is easy to recognize.  Instead, it is about lines, colors, shapes, patterns, and the way paint is applied to the surface.

POP QUIZ

Mark T for true or F for false.

Abstract art is about strange objects.

T / F

▲ Kandinsky's first abstract watercolor painting

KEY WORDS

- strange
- object
- canvas
- puzzle

- solve
- skull
- forever
- abstract

- recognize
- apply
- surface

Wassily Kandinsky was a Russian artist, who painted *Painting on Light Ground* in 1916. 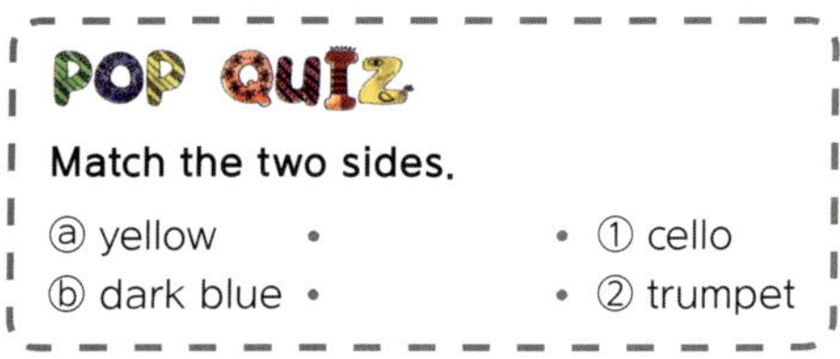

Kandinsky believed that each color represented an emotion.

He also linked each color to the sound of a musical instrument.

Yellow was an exciting trumpet fanfare and green was a peaceful violin. Dark blue was the deep, thoughtful sound of a cello.

Perhaps you can imagine how this painting would sound if it was a piece of music!

KEY WORDS

- Russian
- link A to B
- trumpet fanfare
- peaceful
- thoughtful
- piece

Another famous abstract painter was Piet Mondrian, a Dutch
artist born in 1872.

To begin with, he painted trees and scenes from nature. Then,
in 1911, he moved to France and his paintings began to change.
He still painted natural scenes, but there were more geometric
shapes in them.

This painting, *Gray Tree*, is a good example.

Mondrian went home to the Netherlands in 1914, and had to stay there when the First World War broke out.

He began to experiment with lines and colors, and produced the paintings for which he is most well known. Each one has a white background. On top of this is a grid of vertical and horizontal black lines. Between the lines, some areas are painted in the three primary colors: red, blue and yellow.

The painting below is called *Composition II in Red, Blue and Yellow*.

KEY WORDS

- to begin with
- geometric
- the Netherlands
- **break out** (break-broke-broken)
- experiment

- grid
- vertical (↔ horizontal)
- primary
- composition

Chapter Three

Comprehension Quiz

A The following sentences are about how Munch got the idea for *The Scream*.
Put the sentences in the right order.

❶ I paused, feeling exhausted, and leaned on the fence.

❷ I was walking along the road with two friends.

❸ I sensed an infinite scream passing through nature.

❹ I stood there while my friends walked on.

________ → ________ → ________ → ________

B The following sentences are about *The Ambassadors*. Fill in each blank
with the right word(s) below.

hymn book	globe	lute	skull

❶ The _________ shows that the men were interested in traveling.

❷ The _________ shows that the men were interested in music.

❸ The _________ shows that the men were interested in religion.

❹ The _________ minds us that people do not live forever.

Choose the best answer to each question.

❶ How does *Sunflowers* show life and death?

   a) Some of the flowers are large and some are small.

   b) Some of the flowers have petals on them and some have lost their petals.

   c) Some of the flowers are painted yellow and some are painted black.

   d) Some of the flowers are in a vase and some are on the table.

❷ What is "abstract art"?

   a) art in which the meaning is shown through scenes of nature

   b) art in which the meaning is shown through hidden symbols

   c) art in which the meaning is shown through patterns and colors

   d) art in which there is no meaning at all

❸ What did Kandinsky's colors represent? Choose two answers.

   a) scents in nature   b) musical sounds

   c) geometric shapes   d) human emotions

Codes and Secrets

There are some paintings that may hold deeper secrets. Hidden codes, messages or tricks may be included in a painting. Sometimes the artist has done this on purpose.

▲ Leonardo da Vinci

Sometimes there may not really be a hidden code, but someone looking at the painting sees a pattern or a connection and thinks there is a hidden message. Perhaps the most famous painting in the world is *Mona Lisa*. It was painted by Italian artist Leonardo da Vinci in the early 1500s.

KEY WORDS

- code
- trick
- connection
- Italian

There are many questions to ask about this painting. Who was the woman that da Vinci painted? What is she thinking as she gazes out of the portrait with her famous half-smile?

It is widely agreed that she was Lisa del Giocondo, the wife of a wealthy businessman. But there are some who believe that da Vinci painted *himself* disguised as a woman. However, a deeper secret was revealed in 2010, when experts in Italy magnified parts of the painting. They discovered tiny letters and symbols painted in the picture.

In the right eye are the letters LV, which could simply be the initials of the artist. But there are more letters in the other eye, and the number 72 is hidden in the arch of the bridge in the background.

What do they mean? Nobody knows, but this is not the only da Vinci painting to be so intriguing.

KEY WORDS

- gaze
- widely
- agree
- businessman

- disguise
- reveal
- magnify
- initial

- arch
- intriguing

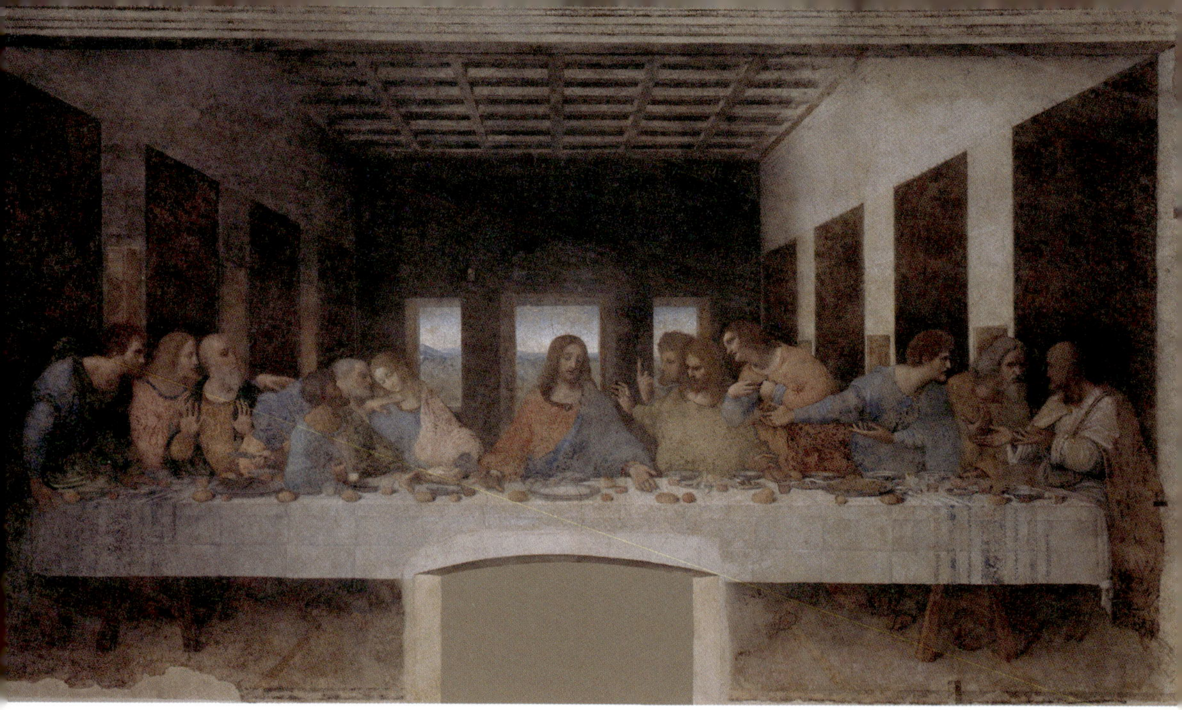

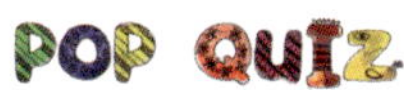

He also painted *The Last Supper*, which is not painted on a canvas, but on the walls of a convent in Milan, Italy. It shows Jesus Christ and his followers sharing a meal on the night before he was killed. It is about 5 m long.

POP QUIZ

What is *The Last Supper* painted on?

ⓐ a canvas

ⓑ a wall

KEY WORDS

- supper
- convent
- Milan
- Jesus Christ
- follower
- share

Each of the followers shows a different emotion on their face.
Jesus has just told them that one of them will betray him.
Their faces show shock, surprise and disbelief.
But some people think that there are hidden secrets in this
painting. None of them have been proved, but still the stories
are passed on and wondered about. This is called *speculation*.

For example, some
people say that the man
sitting on Jesus' right is
not his close friend and
follower, John, but is
actually a woman.

An Italian musician, Giovanni Maria Pala, has made another interesting suggestion. He says that if you look at the positions of all the hands and loaves of bread in the picture, then draw them as musical notes, they form a piece of music. Others think that there are complex mathematical puzzles that predict world disasters. Is this true, or did da Vinci simply paint a picture of a Biblical story? Nobody will ever know, which means that the theories and questions will continue.

▲ notes

POP QUIZ

Mark T for true or F for false.

There are some hidden secrets in *The Last Supper*. Many experts have already proved them.   T / F

KEY WORDS

- make a suggestion
- position
- loaves
- note
- form
- complex
- mathematical
- predict
- disaster
- Biblical
- theory
- continue

Another famous painting on an Italian building is Michelangelo's
The Creation of Adam. This was painted on the ceiling of the
Sistine Chapel in Rome in 1512, and can still be seen today.
It shows God giving life to the first man. Their fingers are close
but not touching, indicating that God is not the same as man,
and is a higher being.

KEY WORDS

- creation
- ceiling
- Sistine Chapel
- indicate
- higher being

Michelangelo studied human anatomy.

Some people think that the shape of the red cloth around God represents the human brain. It is the same shape as a brain, and all the other details accurately show nerves and sections of the brain. The trailing blue cloth seems to be the shape of a major artery in the human brain.

KEY WORDS

- anatomy
- accurately
- nerve
- section
- artery

A painting where the hidden meanings were certainly put there on purpose is *Netherlandish Proverbs*. It was painted in 1559 by Dutch artist Pieter Bruegel.

A proverb is sometimes known as an "idiom." This is a group of words which has a special meaning. The meaning is much different than the dictionary definition of each word.

For example, "over the moon" does not mean to be above the moon. Instead, it means to be very excited and happy.

There are around 112 idioms illustrated in this painting. Some of them are still in use today, in the English language.

One of them is "swimming against the tide." This means to do the opposite of what everyone else is doing. Another is "banging one's head against a brick wall." This means to be extremely frustrated. Can you find them in the picture?

There are a few idioms here that are not generally used in modern times, such as "having one's roof tiled with tarts." This meant having plenty of everything.

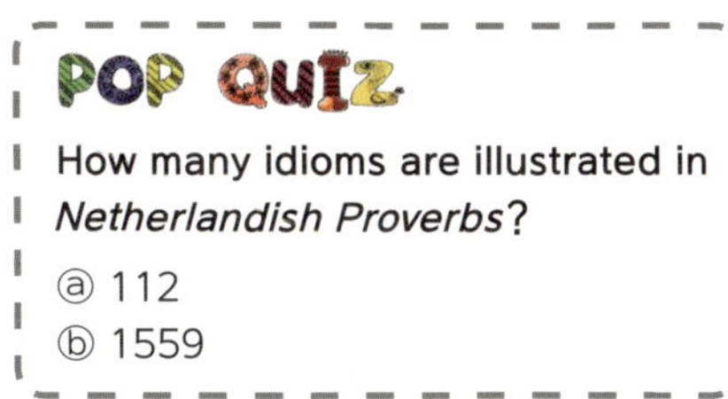

KEY WORDS

- Netherlandish
- proverb
- idiom
- dictionary
- definition
- illustrate

- in use
- language
- tide
- opposite
- else
- bang

- extremely
- frustrated
- tile
- tart
- plenty of

Sometimes the most interesting thing about a painting is what is *not* in the picture.

This painting, *A Monk and Guy's Widow Conversing with the Soul of Guy de Thurno*, was part of a very old book.

Painted in 1475 by Simon Marmion, it shows a group of rather frightened-looking people standing in a circle, looking at something that isn't there!

What are they looking at? The clue is in the title.

The woman's husband, Guy de Thurno, has died and come back in the form of a ghost. Because the ghost is invisible, you can't see it, so you must imagine what it might look and sound like.

Now that you have learned a little about paintings and their hidden meanings, perhaps you could visit an art gallery and see some for yourself. You never know what you might discover…

In *A Monk and Guy's Widow Conversing with the Soul of Guy de Thurno*, what are the people looking at?

ⓐ a book
ⓑ a ghost

KEY WORDS

- monk
- widow
- converse with

- rather
- frightened
- in a circle

- ghost
- invisible (↔ visible)

Chapter Four

Comprehension Quiz

A Connect each painting and painter correctly.

Netherlandish Proverbs

• a) Leonardo da Vinci

A Monk and Guy's Widow Conversing with the Soul of Guy de Thurno

• b) Michelangelo

The Creation of Adam

• c) Pieter Bruegel

The Last Supper

• d) Simon Marmion

B Mark T for true or F for false.

❶ An artist may deliberately include a secret code in a painting. T F

❷ All paintings contain a secret message or meaning. T F

❸ Some people see a pattern or code where there isn't one. T F

Choose the best answer to each question.

❶ Where is the number 72 hidden in *Mona Lisa*?

a) in the woman's right eye

b) in the woman's left eye

c) in the arch of the bridge

d) in the folds of the woman's clothing

❷ What does Giovanni Maria Pala suggest about *The Last Supper*?

a) that the figure to Jesus' right is really Leonardo da Vinci dressed as a woman

b) that the loaves of bread spell out a secret message

c) that the position of Jesus' hands predicts a world disaster

d) that the hands and loaves of bread represent a piece of music

❸ Why do the people in *A Monk and Guy's Widow Conversing with the Soul of Guy de Thurno* look frightened?

a) They are committing a crime.

b) They are looking at a ghost.

c) They are killing someone.

d) They are in prison.

Let's Review the Story

Fill in the blanks to review the story.

Title: Hidden ____________ of Famous ____________

Chapter 1

- **Title:** Paintings of ____________ Life
- **Main Idea:** H____________ know what life used to be like by looking at old drawings, ____________ and sculptures.

Chapter 2

- **Title:** The ____________ World
- **Main Idea:** Many artists have been inspired by p____________, a____________, and other ____________ of nature. This includes the ____________, who painted quickly outdoors to capture a scene.

Chapter 3

- **Title:** E____________ and Meanings
- **Main Idea:** Some artists use c____________, s____________, p____________, and symbols to represent different ____________ and to make people think deeply about things.

Chapter 4

- **Title:** ____________ and Secrets
- **Main Idea:** There are s____________, c____________, and messages ____________ in some paintings, but the meanings are not always clear.

Let's Think & Talk

Think about the following questions and answer them freely.

❶ Among the paintings in the book, which painting do you like the most? Why?

❷ What is *Impressionism* and what is *abstract art*? Explain both of them using a representative painting as an example.

❸ What secrets are hidden in Leonardo da Vinci's paintings? Organize them and tell others what they are.

❹ Do you know any secrets hidden in famous paintings? Search for paintings that have secrets other than the famous paintings that are in the book and tell others what they are.

Let's Review the Story

Title: Hidden **Secrets** of Famous **Paintings**

Chapter 1

- Title: Paintings of **Everyday** Life
- Main Idea: **Historians** know what life used to be like by looking at old drawings, **paintings** and sculptures.

Chapter 2

- Title: The **Natural** World
- Main Idea: Many artists have been inspired by **plants**, **animals**, and other **scenes** of nature. This includes the **Impressionists**, who painted quickly outdoors to capture a scene.

Chapter 3

- Title: **Emotions** and Meanings
- Main Idea: Some artists use **colors**, **shapes**, **patterns**, and symbols to represent different **emotions** and to make people think deeply about things.

Chapter 4

- Title: **Codes** and Secrets
- Main Idea: There are **secrets**, **codes**, and messages **hidden** in some paintings, but the meanings are not always clear.

Smart Readers: **Wise** & **Wide**

After-reading Test

- Hidden Secrets of Famous Paintings
- Level 5
- 27 Questions

  (Vocabulary 7 / Reading Comprehension 16 /

  Sentence Structure & Grammar 4)

1. What does "independent" mean?
   ① not relying on anyone else
   ② not allowing people to be slaves
   ③ celebrating with food and drink
   ④ fighting against other nations

2. What does "voyage" mean?
   ① a ship
   ② a journey by sea
   ③ a vacation
   ④ an experiment

3. Which of the following is the wrong past tense form of the verb?
   ① hung
   ② sold
   ③ lost
   ④ hided

※ Choose the right word for each blank. (4~5)

4. Edouard Manet was suffering _________ a long illness in 1882.
   ① to
   ② off
   ③ from
   ④ with

5. To begin ___________, he painted trees and scenes from nature.
   ① up
   ② of
   ③ into
   ④ with

6.
> • Close up, the painting is made up _______ rough strokes.
> • The dress is richly patterned and her hair appears to be full _______ jewels.

① on   ② of
③ for   ④ into

7.
> • There are two globes, one showing the earth and another that is related _______ the stars.
> • He also linked each color _______ the sound of a musical instrument.

① to   ② off
③ from   ④ above

8. In *A Woman Preparing Bread and Butter for a Boy*, why is the woman preparing bread and butter for the boy?
① He is having supper before he goes to bed.
② He is having breakfast before he goes to school.
③ He has come home from school to have his lunch.
④ He is taking the bread and butter to school with him.

9. What was unusual about John Lewis Krimmel's paintings?
① He included people in his paintings.
② He included free black people in his paintings.
③ He included slaves in his paintings.
④ He included buildings in his paintings.

10. Which of these artists was NOT an Impressionist?
  ① Monet   ② van Gogh
  ③ Krimmel   ④ Renoir

11. How do experts know that Monet's painting of Camille at Trouville and
    others painted at the same time were painted on the beach?
  ① There are grains of sand in the paint.
  ② There are seashells in the paint.
  ③ There is salt in the paint.
  ④ There is sea water in the paint.

12. In *The Great Wave off Kanagawa*, what does Mount Fuji look like?
  ① a wave   ② a boat
  ③ a fish   ④ a cloud

13. What was special about the voyage of HMS Investigator?
  ① The ship had no captain.
  ② There were lots of flowers on board the ship.
  ③ The ship never returned from the voyage.
  ④ It was the first time anyone had ever sailed around Australia.

14. Why didn't Manet paint his pictures outside, like other Impressionists?
  ① He preferred to use a studio.
  ② He thought the light was better indoors.
  ③ He was ill in bed and couldn't go out.
  ④ He was afraid to go outside.

15. What was Munch's original title for *The Scream*?
  ① *The Boardwalk*
  ② *Sunset Scream*
  ③ *The Scream of Nature*
  ④ *Red Sky Over a Bridge*

16. In *Sunflowers*, which of these things did the sunflower NOT represent?
  ① happiness ② devotion
  ③ loyalty ④ fear

17. In *Woman Reading a Letter*, why does the woman in the chair have so little hair?
  ① She has an illness that has made her hair fall out.
  ② She plucked her hair out to make her hat fit better.
  ③ She is following the fashion of the time.
  ④ She was born without any hair.

18. In *Woman Reading a Letter*, what does the single curl of hair on the woman's forehead mean?
  ① that she is married
  ② that she never wants to be married
  ③ that she was married but her husband died
  ④ that she is engaged to be married

19. In *Man Writing a Letter*, who might the man be writing to?
  ① his mother
  ② his sister
  ③ his friend
  ④ his sweetheart

20. What is famous about *Mona Lisa*?
   ① the woman's hair
   ② the woman's hands
   ③ the woman's half-smile
   ④ the woman's eyes

21. Who are the people in *The Last Supper*?
   ① diners at a restaurant
   ② followers of Jesus Christ
   ③ people who live in a convent
   ④ priests in a church

22. In *The Creation of Adam*, why don't the fingers of God and Adam touch each other?
   ① to show that humans were not created by God
   ② to show that God is much greater than humans
   ③ to show that humans are more powerful than God
   ④ to show that God is simply an idea in the human brain

23. What did Michelangelo study?
   ① anatomy   ② history
   ③ geography   ④ chemistry

※ Choose the wrong part of each sentence. (24~26)

24.
You can <u>enjoy</u> and <u>understand</u> a painting <u>very more</u> *if* you know
      ①   ②   ③

something <u>about</u> it.
     ④

25.
All these things <u>make</u> her <u>appears</u> to be <u>bigger</u> than she would
         ①   ②   ③

naturally <u>be</u>.
   ④

26.
<u>In</u> this way, he was <u>able to</u> <u>choosing</u> exactly what <u>to put</u> in the picture.
①   ② ③   ④

27. What is the correct sentence?
   ① It is a picture of a tree, which suggests something long lasting and secure.
   ② It is a picture of a tree, which suggests long lasting something and secure.
   ③ It is a picture of a tree, that suggests long lasting and secure something.
   ④ It is a picture of a tree, that suggests long lasting something and secure.

[Image Credit]

p.13   *Boulevard du Temple* by Louis Daguerre
Louis Daguerre (1787 – 1851) [Public domain], via Wikimedia Commons

p.15   *A Woman Preparing Bread and Butter for a Boy* by Pieter de Hooch
By Hooch, Pieter de (1629 – 1684) (Dutch) (artist, Details of artist on Google Art Project)
[Public domain], via Wikimedia Commons

p.7, 17   *The Laundress* by Jean-Baptiste Greuze
By Jean-Baptiste Greuze (French, 1725 – 1805) (1725 – 1805) (French) (artist, Details of
artist on Google Art Project) [Public domain], via Wikimedia Commons

p.18   *Self-portrait* by Jean-Baptiste Greuze
Jean-Baptiste Greuze (1725 – 1805) [Public domain], via Wikimedia Commons

p.20   *Fourth of July in Center Square* by John Lewis Krimmel
John Lewis Krimmel (1786 – 1821) [Public domain or Public domain], via Wikimedia Commons

p.22   *The Ditchley Portrait* by Marcus Gheeraerts the Younger
Marcus Gheeraerts the Younger (1561/1562 – 1636) [Public domain], via Wikimedia Commons

p.25   ① *Haystacks* by Claude Monet
Claude Monet (1840 – 1926) [Public domain], via Wikimedia Commons

② *Dance at Le Moulin de la Galette* by Pierre-Auguste Renoir
Pierre-Auguste Renoir (1841 – 1919) [Public domain], via Wikimedia Commons

③ *The Luncheon on the Grass* by Edouard Manet
Édouard Manet (1832 – 1883) [Public domain], via Wikimedia Commons

④ *Dancer with a Bouquet of Flowers* by Edgar Degas
Edgar Degas (1834 – 1917) [Public domain or Public domain], via Wikimedia Commons

p.26   *Camille on the Beach at Trouville* by Claude Monet
Claude Monet (1840 – 1926) [Public domain], via Wikimedia Commons

p.33   *The Great Wave off Kanagawa* by Katsushika Hokusai
Katsushika Hokusai (葛飾北斎) (1760 – 1849) [Public domain], via Wikimedia Commons

p.34–35   *A Thousand Li of Rivers and Mountains* by Wang Ximeng
By Wang Ximeng (王希孟) (1096 – 1119) (http://guoxue.zynews.com/XianFeng/2008/2202.html)
[Public domain], via Wikimedia Commons

p.36   *Tiger in a Tropical Storm (Surprised)* by Henri Rousseau
Henri Rousseau (1844 – 1910) [Public domain], via Wikimedia Commons

p.39   *A Hare in the Forest* by Hans Hoffmann
By Hans Hoffmann (German, about 1530 – 1591/1592) (1530 – 1592) (German)
(artist, Details of artist on Google Art Project) [Public domain], via Wikimedia Commons

p.41   *Cypripedium calceolus* by Franz Bauer
By Franz Bauer (1758 – 1840) (a copy of which was here) [Public domain or Public domain],
via Wikimedia Commons

p.43   *Banksia coccinea* by Ferdinand Bauer
By Ferdinand Bauer (1760 – 1826) [Public domain], via Wikimedia Commons

p.7, 44   *Lilac in a Glass* by Edouard Manet
Édouard Manet (1832 – 1883) [Public domain], via Wikimedia Commons

Sarah J. Dodd
Sarah J. Dodd is an experienced primary school teacher who resides in the UK, but has also lived and taught in Australia. She has a PhD in Science and a certificate in Creative Writing. She has published several books for children: "An Angel Anyway" (Anyway Press, 2008), the "Little Angels" series (Lion Children's Books, 2009/10), "The Lion Picture Bible" (Lion Children's Books, 2015) and "Legs: the tale of a meerkat lost and found" (Lion Children's Books, 2015). Her poetry for children has also been highly commended and published in the anthology "Let in the Stars" (Manchester Metropolitan University, 2014).
She is currently working on further picture books for the very young, and a novel for older children.

Hidden Secrets of Famous Paintings

Written by Sarah J. Dodd
Illustrated by Sohyeon Lee

First Published in March 2016

Editorial Manager: Juyon Choi
Editors: Kyunghee Jang, Juyon Choi, Jiyeong Park
Designer: Eunhee Lee
Cover Designer: Eunhee Lee

Published and distributed by

Darakwon Bldg., 64-1 Jandari-ro, Mapo-gu, Seoul, Korea 04031
Tel: 82-2-736-2031(ext. 250)   Fax: 82-2-732-2037
Homepage: www.ihappyhouse.co.kr
Publisher: Kyudo Chung

ISBN: 978-89-6653-294-0 18740 / 978-89-6653-156-1 18740(set)

[Components]
• 1 Audio CD (Recording Studio: Aram)
• Answer Keys & Korean Translation: Free download at www.ihappyhouse.co.kr